WONDERS OF CANADA

L'Anse aux Meadows

Carol Koopmans

Weigl

CALGARY
www.weigl.com

Published by Weigl Educational Publishers Limited
6325 10th Street SE
Calgary, Alberta
T2H 2Z9

Website: www.weigl.com

We acknowledge the financial support of the Government of Canada through the Book Publishing
Industry Development Program (BPIDP) for our publishing activities.

Library and Archives Cataloguing in Publication

Koopmans, Carol
        L'Anse aux Meadows / Carol Koopmans.

(Wonders of Canada)
Includes index.
ISBN 978-1-55388-387-6 (bound)
ISBN 978-1-55388-388-3 (pbk.)

    1. L'Anse aux Meadows National Historic Site (N.L.)—Juvenile literature. 2. World
Heritage areas--Newfoundland and Labrador--Juvenile literature. I. Title. II. Series.
FC2164.L36K66 2007   j971.8   C2007-902257-X

Printed in the United States of America
1 2 3 4 5 6 7 8 9 0 11 10 09 08 07

Photograph Credits

Every reasonable effort has been made to trace ownership and to obtain
permission to reprint copyright material. The publishers would be pleased to
have any errors or omissions brought to their attention so that they may be
corrected in subsequent printings.

© **Barrett & McKay Photo**: pages 10 and 19 bottom middle; **courtesy of
Carol Koopmans**: pages 1, 3, 5, and 21 bottom; **Parks Canada**: pages 4
(H.01.11.01.04[40]), and 19 bottom left (H.01.11.06.15[01])

All of the Internet URLs given in the book were valid at the time of publication.
However, due to the dynamic nature of the Internet, some addresses may have
changed, or sites may have ceased to exist since publication. While the author
and publisher regret any inconvenience this may cause readers, no responsibility
for any such changes can be accepted by either the author or the publisher.

Project Coordinator
Leia Tait

Design
Terry Paulhus

Contents

Village of Discovery

Imagine a village more than 1,000 years old. Sod houses stand low on the horizon. Ancient objects from the past lay buried underground. Cold waves crash against a rocky beach.

This is L'Anse aux Meadows in the province of Newfoundland and Labrador. L'Anse aux Meadows is the site of a **Norse** village that was built around the year 1,000 AD. This is the only Norse settlement in North America outside of Greenland. It is also the oldest European settlement in North America. The house ruins and other objects uncovered here prove that the Norse arrived in this part of the Americas more than 500 years before Christopher Columbus. This makes L'Anse aux Meadows an important place in Norse, Canadian, and world history. To protect this history, L'Anse aux Meadows was made a World Heritage Site in 1978.

▬ The sod buildings at L'Anse aux Meadows today have been rebuilt to look like those that stood at the site 1,000 years ago.

What is a World Heritage Site?

Heritage is what people inherit from those who lived before them. It is also what they pass down to future generations. Heritage is made up of many things. Objects, traditions, beliefs, values, places, and people are all part of heritage. Throughout history, these things have been **preserved**. A family's heritage is preserved in the stories, customs, and objects its members pass on to each other. Similarly, a common human heritage is preserved in the beliefs, objects, and places that have special meaning for all people, such as L'Anse aux Meadows.

The United Nations Educational, Scientific and Cultural Organization (UNESCO) identifies places around the world that are important to all people. Some are important places in nature. Others are related to **culture**. These landmarks become World Heritage Sites. They are protected from being destroyed by **urbanization,** pollution, tourism, and neglect.

▬ **Boats like those once used by the Norse are found at L'Anse aux Meadows today.**

You can learn more about UNESCO World Heritage Sites by visiting **http://whc.unesco.org**.

▶Think about it◀

World Heritage Sites belong to all people. They provide a link to the past. These sites also help people from many cultures connect with each other. Think about your own heritage. What landmarks are important to you? Think about the places that have shaped your life. Make a list of your personal heritage sites. The list might include your home, your grandparents' home, your school, or any other place that is special to you and your family. Next to each location on the list, write down why it is important to you.

Where in the World?

L'Anse aux Meadows is located at the northernmost tip of the island of Newfoundland. Labrador, on the mainland, can be seen on the horizon. The site overlooks Epavés Bay, a shallow body of water in the North Atlantic Ocean.

The village at L'Anse aux Meadows is nestled on a small, grassy hill near the shore. The village once had at least eight buildings. These included a large hall, two smaller houses, and some workshops. Three of these structures have been rebuilt. The largest is 21 metres long, with different rooms for eating and sleeping. A traditional fence of woven branches encloses the main village area. Outside the fence are a **smithy** and a fire pit. A small stream called Black Duck Brook runs past the village. The stream begins from a lake 2 kilometres inland and empties into the bay just beyond the village. Behind the stream is a stretch of marshland, called a bog.

■ **L'Anse aux Meadows sits on the Great Northern Peninsula. This is a piece of land that juts out into the Atlantic Ocean and is almost completely surrounded by water. It is known as a rugged region.**

Puzzler

The first Norse explorers came from Iceland and Greenland. **Historians** believe they sailed west from their homelands toward what is now Baffin Island. They turned south to follow the coast of present-day Labrador. The Norse travelled on to Newfoundland, where they stopped to build a settlement at what is today L'Anse aux Meadows. From there, the Norse may have made voyages through the Gulf of St. Lawrence to what are now Nova Scotia and New Brunswick, and further down the Atlantic coast. Use the route drawn on the map to match the letters with the locations listed below.

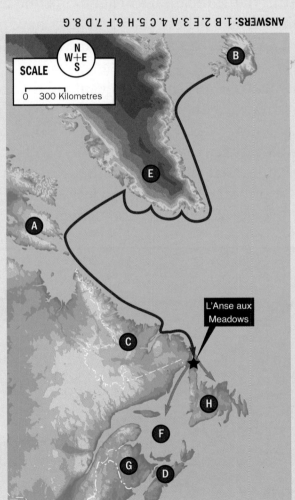

ANSWERS: 1. B 2. E 3. A 4. C 5. H 6. F 7. D 8. G

SCALE

0   300 Kilometres

L'Anse aux Meadows

1. Iceland

2. Greenland

3. Baffin Island

4. Labrador

5. Newfoundland

6. Gulf of St. Lawrence

7. Nova Scotia

8. New Brunswick

A Trip Back in Time

Around 1,000 AD, explorer Leif Ericsson set sail from Greenland. He was searching for land a trader named Bjarni Herjulfsson had seen 15 years earlier. Leif and his crew of 35 men sailed for many days. They landed at present-day L'Anse aux Meadows. The Norse built sod houses and spent the winter exploring the area. Leif called the place *Vinland*. Most historians believe this name means "Wineland," for the wild berries Leif's men found at the site. Others believe the name may have come from the Norwegian word for "pasture," because of the meadows the crew found in the area.

Leif and his crew returned to Greenland the following year. During the next 20 years, many Norse groups lived at L'Anse aux Meadows. They rested at the site during long voyages and used it as a base for exploring inland. During these explorations, the Norse met the Beothuk. This was an **Aboriginal** group that hunted and fished in the area. They co-operated at first, but conflict soon forced the Norse to leave. For this reason, L'Anse aux Meadows did not become a permanent settlement. The Norse left the area by 1050.

■ Leif Ericsson and his crew sailed to Vinland in a boat that had belonged to Bjarni Herjulfsson. When they neared what is now Newfoundland and Labrador, Leif and his men became excited.

Site Science

The Norse were skilled metalworkers. They might have chosen the site of L'Anse aux Meadows because of the presence of bog iron. Streams flowing into bogs often carry dissolved iron particles. Chemicals and **bacteria** in the bog cause the iron to separate from the water and form tiny balls. The Norse collected these balls from the bog at L'Anse aux Meadows. They heated the iron in a large, clay furnace fuelled with charcoal. Temperatures inside the furnace could reach 1,300° Celsius. The heat helped remove impurities from the iron. This process, called smelting, took many hours. It made the iron sponge-like. Blacksmiths then removed the iron from the furnace and continued to heat it over a fire until it was soft. While the iron was still warm, the smiths shaped it into metal nails, bolts, tools, weapons, and other items.

▬ Today, Norse metalworking is demonstrated by blacksmiths at L'Anse aux Meadows.

FIND MORE ONLINE

Learn more about Norse metalworking at www.regia.org/life/ironwork.htm.

Becoming a World Heritage Site

For hundreds of years, no one knew of the Norse settlement at L'Anse aux Meadows. Vinland was remembered in Norse tales, called **sagas**, but no one knew its exact location. Many people questioned whether Vinland really existed.

Norwegian historian Helge Ingstad studied the sagas. Based on clues found in these tales, Helge believed Vinland was in North America. In 1960, Helge and his wife, Anne, travelled to Newfoundland and Labrador. They began digging in some unusual mounds of dirt found at L'Anse aux Meadows. Helge and Anne uncovered the remains of a Norse village. Historians believe this is the settlement Leif Ericsson built more than 1,000 years ago in Vinland.

The discovery proved Norse explorers had arrived in this part of North America 500 years before any other European. This made L'Anse aux Meadows an important historic site. Many people wanted to ensure the Norse ruins would be preserved for the future. UNESCO named L'Anse aux Meadows a World Heritage Site on August 9, 1985.

■ **The Norse ruins at L'Anse aux Meadows are the oldest European remains in North America.**

Heritage Heroes

Helge Ingstad was born in Norway. As a young man, he worked as a lawyer. In 1926, Helge decided to become an explorer in the Northwest Territories. For three years, he lived and travelled with an Aboriginal group there. Afterward, Helge returned to Norway. He wrote a book about his adventures, called *The Land of Feast and Famine.* Over the next few years, Helge travelled to Alaska, Arizona, Greenland, Iceland, and Mexico. He often returned to Norway to publish books about his many adventures.

In 1941, Helge met and married Anne Stine. Anne was an **archaeologist**. Together, Helge and Anne travelled the world, studying history and culture. The Norse settlement at L'Anse aux Meadows was their most important discovery. From 1961 to 1968, Helge and Anne led an **excavation** of the site. They found many items, such as rusty nails, a bronze pin, a stone lamp, and a bone needle. They also found a spindle whorl made of stone. This was a tool Norse women used to spin wool. It proved that women once lived at the settlement.

■ On September 5, 1963, Helge Ingstad officially announced the discovery of a Norse settlement at L'Anse aux Meadows.

World Heritage in
CANADA

There are more than 800 UNESCO World Heritage Sites in 138 countries around the globe. Canada has 14 of these sites. Seven are natural sites, and seven are cultural sites. Each is believed to be of outstanding heritage value to all people around the world. Look at the map. Are any of these sites near your home? Have you visited any of them? Learn more about World Heritage Sites in Canada by visiting www.pc.gc.ca/progs/spm-whs/itm2-/index_e.asp.

Dinosaur Provincial Park (Alberta)
- One of the largest and most important collections of dinosaur fossils in the world

Head-Smashed-In Buffalo Jump (Alberta)
- A large, ancient cliff once used by the Plains Aboriginal Peoples to hunt bison on the Prairies
- One of the oldest and best-preserved buffalo jumps in North America

Rideau Canal (Ontario)
- The best-preserved example of a slackwater canal in North America
- The only 19th-century North American canal that is still in use

1 Canadian Rocky Mountain Parks
(Alberta and British Columbia)

2 Dinosaur Provincial Park (Alberta)

3 Gros Morne National Park
(Newfoundland and Labrador)

4 Head-Smashed-In Buffalo
Jump (Alberta)

5   The Historic District of
    Old-Quebec (Quebec)

6   Kluane/Wrangell-St Elias/Glacier
    Bay/Tatshenshini-Alsek (British
    Columbia, Yukon, and Alaska)

7   L'Anse aux Meadows National
    Historic Site (Newfoundland
    and Labrador)

8   Miguasha National Park (Quebec)

9   Nahanni National Park Reserve
    (Northwest Territories)

10   Old Town Lunenburg (Nova Scotia)

11   Rideau Canal (Ontario)

12   SGang Gwaay (British Columbia)

13   Waterton Glacier International
    Peace Park (Alberta and Montana)

14   Wood Buffalo National Park
    (Alberta and Northwest Territories)

Natural Wonders

The climate at L'Anse aux Meadows was mild 1,000 years ago. There was little snow during the winter. Summer temperatures could be quite hot. Over time, this changed. Temperatures became cooler. Today, the Labrador Current has a strong effect on weather at L'Anse aux Meadows. The current is a flow of cold water from the Arctic. It moves southeast along the coast of Newfoundland and Labrador, causing temperatures to drop below zero during the winter. Arctic icebergs drifting in the current are a common sight.

Despite the cool climate, more than 280 different plants grow in the region around L'Anse aux Meadows. These include more than 90 **species** of herbs, more than 60 types of trees and shrubs, and a large number of ferns, mosses, lichens, and liverworts. Many flowers, grasses, and berries also grow here. Caribou, moose, and other animals make their homes in nearby forests of small trees and shrubs, called tuckamore.

▬ **Iceberg watching is a favourite pastime of many visitors to the L'Anse aux Meadows area.**

FIND MORE ONLINE

Learn more about icebergs in Newfoundland and Labrador at **http://icebergfinder.com**.

Creature Feature

Caribou have lived in what is now Newfoundland and Labrador for thousands of years. They were important to the Beothuk people who once lived in the area. The Beothuk ate caribou meat and made clothing and shelter from the animals' hides. The Beothuk groups that the Norse met near L'Anse aux Meadows may have been following the caribou herds. The herds **migrate** to the northern part of the province each summer. In the sagas about Vinland, the Norse described large numbers of caribou-like animals, which they called *dyr*. Like the Beothuk, the Norse hunted these animals for food and hides.

■ The caribou has become a special symbol of Newfoundland and Labrador.

Caribou belong to the deer family. All caribou have antlers, small ears, and long, slim legs. Their brown fur helps them blend into natural settings. This makes it difficult for **predators** to see them. Caribou are found in every province except New Brunswick and Nova Scotia. Today, 500,000 caribou live in Newfoundland and Labrador. This is half of all the caribou in Canada.

Cultural Treasures

In 1,000 AD, the Norse were known throughout the world as fierce warriors, skilled sailors, and master shipbuilders. They were clever traders and brave explorers. In their homelands, the Norse were known to be expert farmers. They planted crops and tended herds of cattle, goats, and sheep. They were also respected **artisans**. Women wove fine woollen fabrics. Norse carpenters, wood carvers, and jewellers crafted beautiful pieces from wood and metal.

Few traces of Norse culture survived in Newfoundland and Labrador. However, the discovery of L'Anse aux Meadows created a strong interest in Norse culture. Today, the only route to L'Anse aux Meadows is along the Viking Trail. This is a themed highway that celebrates Norse culture. Traditional foods, such as *lefse*, are served at Norse restaurants along the trail. Shops sell Norse art and handicrafts. Festivals and special events are held in the area throughout the year to celebrate Norse culture with music, dancing, storytelling, and theatre.

▬ **The period from the eighth to the eleventh centuries is remembered as the Great Age of the Norse. Museums around the world display metal armour and other objects from this period.**

Telling Tales

Norse sagas were passed down orally for hundreds of years. Most were not written down until the thirteenth century. Among the many tales remembered in the sagas is Leif Ericsson's discovery of Vinland.

Leif and his crew sailed for two days before seeing land. Heading toward it, they came to an island. The men went ashore. The weather was fine, and there was dew on the grass. The sailors caught the dew in their hands and brought it to their mouths to drink. They had never tasted anything so sweet.

Leif led the men back to their ship. They sailed around the island until they came into shallow water near the shore of the land. The adventurers could not wait to set foot on the land. They jumped into the water and ran to shore. The men found a river running from a large lake to the ocean. They returned to their ship. When the tide rose, Leif and his crew sailed up the river to the lake.

Leif and his crew took their belongings from the ship and began exploring. The river and lake were full of the largest salmon the explorers had ever seen. The land was rich, with many pastures. Leif decided they would stay for the winter.

Amazing Attractions

There is much to see and learn at L'Anse aux Meadows. Visitors can explore the site on their own or join a group for a guided tour. Most visits begin in the Visitor Centre. Educational displays teach visitors about L'Anse aux Meadows. Many **artifacts** from the site are on display. A theatre shows films about the site, and a model of the village shows the layout of the site.

Outside, visitors must follow a plank wood path, called the boardwalk, to the village. Here, visitors can enter the sod buildings to see how the Norse lived. **Interpreters** in Norse clothing re-enact the tasks of daily life at the settlement. Some show how to make and use Norse tools. Others sing old Norse songs, tell stories from the sagas, and make traditional foods. Staff members also answer questions and provide visitors with information about the site. They help visitors imagine life at the settlement more than 1,000 years ago.

▬ **Many of the interpreters at L'Anse aux Meadows have Norse heritage. They show visitors what life was like for the Norse who settled at the site.**

Featured Attraction

The sod houses at L'Anse aux Meadows are the site's main attraction. They were built to look like the original dwellings the Norse built at the site. All Norse sod houses were built using the same basic steps. First, the Norse made a frame of wooden beams. They laid blocks of sod over the frame. The blocks were about 20 centimetres thick, 50 centimetres wide, and 150 centimetres long. The sod kept the shelters cool in summer and warm in winter. Long fire pits in the centre of the floor provided heat, light, and fuel for cooking. Openings in the roof let in natural light and allowed smoke from the fire to escape. The floor was made of dirt. Wooden benches along the walls were used for sitting and sleeping.

Issues in Heritage

Preserving heritage at L'Anse aux Meadows can be a challenge. The site is open to the public from June until October. About 30,000 people visit each year. During peak times, many visitors are present on the site at the same time. The Visitor Centre, sod buildings, and boardwalk sometimes become crowded. Large tour buses bringing visitors to and from the site make it difficult for visitors to imagine what the site was like 1,000 years ago. Park staff are finding new ways to handle large numbers of visitors without ruining their experience of the site. To help, tour buses are no longer allowed to park near the ruins.

The site is also affected by disturbances caused by filming. Each year, park staff receive about 15 requests from television and movie crews wanting to film at the site. Many of these crews do not want visitors present when they are filming. They often want to include artifacts from the site in their films. To prevent damage to the site and its artifacts, staff at L'Anse aux Meadows have enforced strict rules for film crews to follow.

▬ **L'Anse aux Meadows is the setting for many films about the Norse.**

Should more film crews be allowed at L'Anse aux Meadows?

YES	NO
Films are another way of teaching people about L'Anse aux Meadows. They are helpful for those who may never have a chance to visit the site.	There are many other ways to learn about L'Anse aux Meadows, such as websites, documentaries, study programs, and books. 
Film crews often pay a great deal of money to film at unique locations. This income could be used to continue excavations, employ more staff, and increase visitor education programs. 	Film crews often want to take artifacts out of their display cases to film up close or to use as props. These priceless objects may be damaged by light and heat from film equipment or by mishandling by film crews.
Allowing the site buildings and artifacts to be filmed helps to ensure that movies and shows about the time period are accurate.	 Filming interrupts visiting hours, reducing the number of people who can visit the site.

Think about this issue. Are there any possible solutions that would satisfy both sides of the debate?

Baking Lefse

Lefse is a traditional Norwegian flatbread that resembles tortillas. It is made from potatoes, milk, eggs, and flour. Norse people often decorate lefse using rolling pins with designs carved on them. With an adult's help, make your own lefse using this recipe. For extra sweetness, serve with butter, sugar, and cinnamon, or strawberry jam.

Materials Needed:
A large pot, a frying pan, a strainer, a knife, a potato peeler, a potato masher, a rolling pin, 10 potatoes, 250 millilitres of white flour, two eggs, and 15 millilitres of butter or margarine

1 Help an adult peel the potatoes and cut them into medium-sized chunks. Add the potatoes to a pot of water, and boil them until they are soft.

2 Ask an adult to drain the potatoes in a strainer. Then, help mash the potatoes with a potato masher. Let them cool.

3 Add the butter and eggs to the mashed potatoes, and stir. Then, add the flour. Stir until the mixture becomes a stiff dough. Chill the dough for several hours.

4 Shape the chilled dough into egg-sized balls. Sprinkle some flour on a counter or table, and use a rolling pin to roll out the balls into flat circles.

5 Ask an adult to fry the circles in a frying pan. Fry each side until golden-brown spots appear.

6 Let the lefse cool, then enjoy.

Quiz

1. When did the Norse first settle at L'Anse aux Meadows?
2. Who discovered the remains of a Norse settlement at L'Anse aux Meadows in 1960?
3. True or false? The Norse sagas have no importance in the history of L'Anse aux Meadows.
4. What feature of the Atlantic Ocean affects the weather at L'Anse aux Meadows?
5. How many tourists visit the historic archaeological site of L'Anse aux Meadows each year?
    a. 100,000   b. 5,000   c. 30,000   d. 1 million

ANSWERS: 1. 1,000 AD   **2.** Helge Ingstad **3.** False. The sagas describe the discovery of Vinland, which led to the discovery of the Norse settlement at L'Anse aux Meadows. **4.** the Labrador Current **5.** c. 30,000

Further Research

You can find more information on L'Anse aux Meadows at your local library or on the Internet.

Libraries

Most libraries have computers that connect to a database for researching information. If you input a key word, you will be provided with a list of books in the library that contain information on that topic. Non-fiction books are arranged numerically, using their call number. Fiction books are organized alphabetically by the author's last name.

Websites

Retrace the Norse voyage to Vinland by clicking "Viking Voyage" at **www.mnh.si.edu/vikings/start.html**.

Explore the Viking Trail at **www.vikingtrail.org/welcome.html**.

Glossary

Aboriginal: the first people who lived in Canada and their descendants, including First Nations, Inuit, and Métis

archaeologist: a scientist who studies objects from the past to learn about the people who made them

artifacts: objects used or made by humans long ago

artisans: workers whose occupations require skill with their hands

bacteria: a group of single-celled microorganisms that live in soil, water, and the bodies of plants and animals

culture: the characteristics, beliefs, and practices of a racial, religious, or social group

excavation: a carefully planned dig to uncover objects buried in the ground

historians: people who study the past

interpreters: people who explain the meaning of something by acting it out

migrate: to move from place to place with the change in weather

Norse: the name given to people from the Scandinavian lands, including Denmark, Norway, Sweden, Iceland, Finland, and Greenland

predators: animals that kill and eat other animals

preserved: protected from injury, loss, or ruin

sagas: tales of historic or legendary people and events in Norway and Iceland

smithy: the workshop of a blacksmith or metalworker

species: a group of plants or animals that share the same characteristics

urbanization: the movement of people out of the countryside and into cities

Index